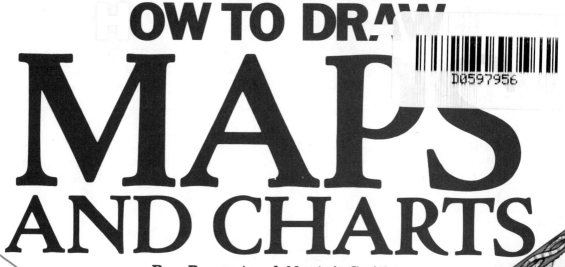

# HOW TO DRAW MAPS AND CHARTS

**Pam Beasant and Alastair Smith**

Edited by Lisa Miles and Judy Tatchell

Designed by Nigel Reece and Fiona Brown

Illustrated by Peter Dennis,
Colin King, Guy Smith and Cathy Simpson

Additional designs by Iain Ashman

SCHOLASTIC INC.
New York  Toronto  London  Auckland  Sydney

## Contents

**Consultant: Rosemary Duncan**

# About this book

Maps and charts are visual ways of showing information. As well as having practical purposes, such as showing a route or a set of facts, maps and charts can also make vivid, attractive pictures.

## About maps

Maps show the outline of an area and its features. Some maps show routes and landmarks. Others show facts, such as how many people live in that area. Below are some aspects of map drawing which are explained later in the book.

### Scale

You can make a map of an area almost any size you like. This technique is called drawing to scale. This is a medium-scale map.

Lake

### Symbols

Maps use symbols to show real features. This saves space and makes them easy to read. The meaning of each symbol is clear.

Beach

### Decoration

Maps can be decorated with intricate patterns, borders and symbolic pictures to add brightness and character.

### Color

Different colors and types of shading can be used to show facts, such as the height of the land, or the depth of the sea.

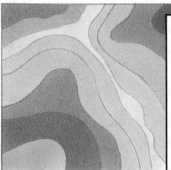

## Professional map production

Professional mapmakers, called cartographers, use great skill and sophisticated computer equipment to make their maps.

Cartographers can even make maps of the surface of the Earth and other planets using pictures taken by satellites and space probes far out in space.

# About charts

Charts show information visually in the form of a diagram, so that it can be understood at a glance. You can choose different types of chart to show your information. For example, both the pie chart and the bar chart below show the number and type of pets owned by a group of people. You can decorate your charts to reflect what they show.

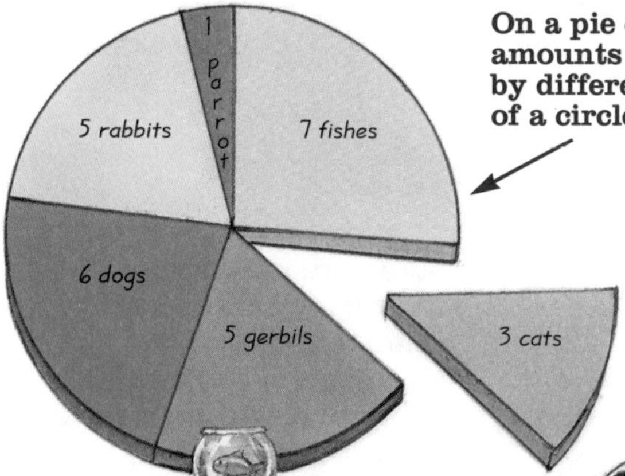

On a pie chart, different amounts are represented by different-sized sections of a circle.

5 rabbits

1 parrot

7 fishes

6 dogs

5 gerbils

3 cats

Bar charts divide up information into blocks. Different amounts are shown by blocks of different heights.

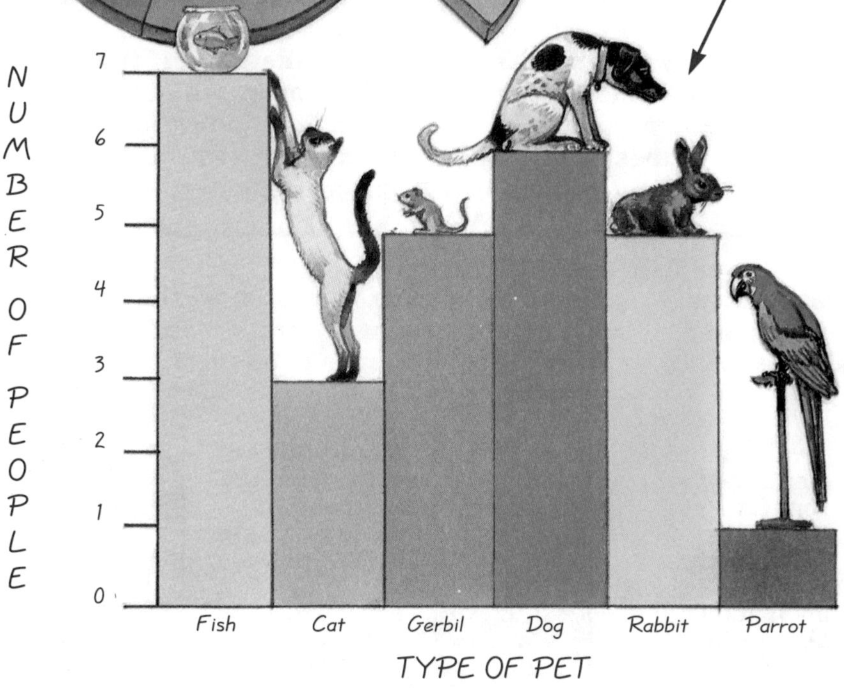

NUMBER OF PEOPLE

7
6
5
4
3
2
1
0

Fish   Cat   Gerbil   Dog   Rabbit   Parrot

TYPE OF PET

*The map on pages 16-17 was done with an airbrush.

## Things to use

You can do the projects in this book using equipment that is cheap and easily available in most art shops. Some useful items are shown here.

You need plain paper for drawing or thicker art paper for painting.

Soft-leaded pencils are good for sketching and shading. Hard-leaded pencils are good for fine lines and detail.

Felt-tip pens and color pencils can be used for most of the maps and charts in this book.

Watercolor paints are useful for large areas of color and an even finish.

A ruler, a pair of compasses and a flexible curve ruler will help you to draw accurate angles and curves.

Many of the maps in this book were done with an artist's airbrush*. A modeller's airbrush is cheaper.

# A basic map

A map showing the area around your home is one of the simplest to draw. As well as main roads, it can include places such as churches and parkland.

Over the next four pages you can find out how to plan a route between your home and a nearby place, such as a friend's house.

## Stage 1: rough sketch

Start by drawing a small square (your home) in one corner of a sheet of paper. Make a rough sketch from memory of all the roads between your house and your friend's house. Draw the map so that it fills your paper. When all the roads are in place, draw your friend's house.

## Stage 2: measuring the roads

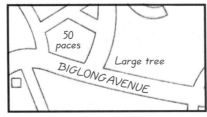

Measure the route by walking along it and counting the number of paces. Note the paces between each junction on your rough map. Plot on the map any landmarks that you see. Sketch any streets that you go past. Note the names of streets that you do not know.

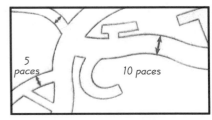

Take care and do not measure while crossing roads. Use standard widths such as five paces for a narrow road and ten for a wider one. Make rough sketches of the angles at which streets meet. You do not need to draw them accurately at this stage.

## Map facts: scale

A map scale tells how much real distance is represented by a distance shown on the map. Once real distances have been measured, a scale is chosen so that the map can be drawn accurately and fitted on the sheet of paper to be used.

Country maps are often small-scale. 1cm (or 1/2in) represents a long distance, such as 50km (about 30 miles).

A road map is medium-scale. 1cm (or 1/2in) stands for less distance than on a small-scale map, such as 2 1/2km (or 1 1/2 miles).

Maps you can draw from the instructions on these pages are large-scale. 1cm (or 1/2in) stands for a short distance, say 50 paces.

## Stage 3: choosing a scale

To choose your scale, add up the number of paces down the longest road you measured. As an example, if the longest street is 500 paces, a good scale might be 1cm = 50 paces (or ½in = 50 paces). On the map, the street would be 10cm, or 5in, long.

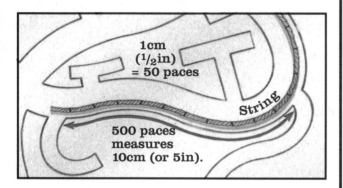

Draw the scaled measurement of the street on some paper and check it to see if you think that your whole map will fit. If the road is curved, you could measure it using a piece of string, marked off in centimetres or half inches.

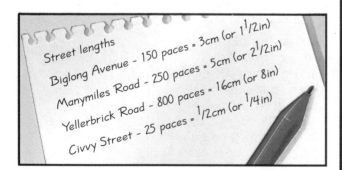

Once you have decided on your scale, convert all your measurements, so that you know how long the roads will need to be. (If you have an awkward number of paces, round them up or down to the nearest ten.)

## Stage 4: north and south

Most maps are drawn so that north is toward the top and south is toward the bottom. North is usually drawn on a map as an arrow with the letter N at the tip.

To find north for your map, stand outside your house. Line up your map road with the direction of the real road.

Using a compass*, find the direction of north and mark it on your map.

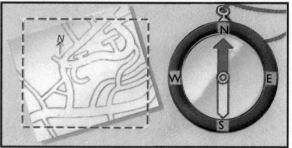

When you draw your map out neatly, north should be at the top. The red lines show how the finished map will be positioned (see page 7).

*You can buy a compass from a camping shop.

## Stage 5: symbols

Most maps use symbols to represent details. This makes them clearer and easier to draw. When you draw your map, decide which symbols you will use to show landmarks. Write a list of all the things you need to show and draw the symbol you will use beside each item. Make each symbol very clear and simple.

In a corner of your map, show all your symbols in a box and write the meanings clearly beside each symbol. This is called a key. The key on the map opposite is in the top left-hand corner.

 Cake shop    Burger bar   Large tree    Library

 Swimming pool    Cinema   Ice rink    Video store

 Spooky house   Bank    Post office   Pond

## Stage 6: drawing the map

1. Using your rough map as a guide, start plotting the roads on tracing paper, using pencil. Begin with a large crossroads, or a similar prominent feature. Add the other major roads.

2. Mark in the side roads (using the string to measure them if they are curved). Make sure that the roads fit together properly.

3. Now position the two houses and landmarks. Use the symbols you have chosen.

Major roads

4. Draw a box for the key and the map title (see **Title boxes** on page 7).

5. Turn the tracing paper over. On the back of the paper, draw over the lines of the map with a pencil.

6. Lay the paper right side up over fresh paper. Go over the lines to transfer them to the fresh paper. Then ink in the lines and color the map.

7. Write in the scale near the edge of the map. (See page 11 for ways to show map scales.)

Scale: 1cm (or ½in) = 50 paces

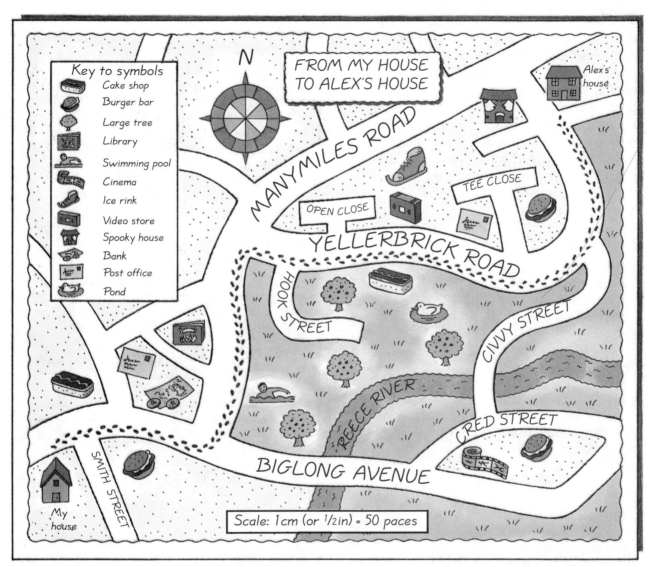

**Key to symbols**

- Cake shop
- Burger bar
- Large tree
- Library
- Swimming pool
- Cinema
- Ice rink
- Video store
- Spooky house
- Bank
- Post office
- Pond

N

FROM MY HOUSE TO ALEX'S HOUSE

Alex's house

MANYMILES ROAD

TEE CLOSE

OPEN CLOSE

YELLERBRICK ROAD

HOOK STREET

CIVVY STREET

REECE RIVER

CRED STREET

BIGLONG AVENUE

SMITH STREET

My house

Scale: 1cm (or ¹/₂in) = 50 paces

## Borders

This map has been drawn with a white border around it. A map border is called a neatline. Alternatively, you could draw your map up to the edge of the paper.

## Title boxes

If you like, you can give your map a title and write it in a title box. Decorated title boxes are called cartouches. You can find out more on page 9.

## Drawing in the route

Your preferred route can be shown in several ways. Footprints show that you can walk there. You could use arrows or an unbroken line instead.

# Showing map details

Maps of the same area can look different depending on the way they are drawn. For example, information about the climate or what types of plants grow in a certain area can be shown as different shades or with a collection of symbols. The examples of map details that appear on these pages show some of the techniques you can use on the projects throughout the book.

## Buildings

On medium-scale maps, simple silhouettes can show the positions of important buildings.

Buildings are plotted in more detail on larger-scale maps. Important buildings are drawn as if you are looking down on them.

## Forests

You can use small tree symbols to represent forests. The closer together the trees are, the denser the forest is. Graded shades of green using coloured pencil can also show the density of trees.*

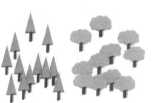

Pine forest    Broadleaved forest

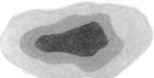

## Showing height

Maps that show land height are called relief maps. Ways of showing height, such as contours (see pages 10-11) may also show steepness.* Lines drawn up and down a hill, called hachures, get thicker as the ground gets steeper.

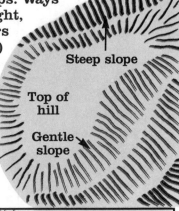

Steep slope

Top of hill

Gentle slope

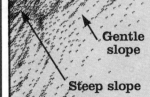

Gentle slope

Steep slope

A technique called stippling uses small dots. They are closer together as the hill gets steeper.

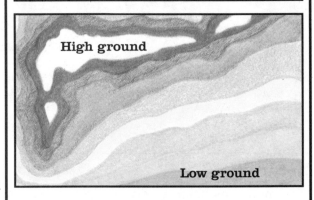

High ground

Low ground

You can use layers of shade to show different heights. Usually, the lowest ground is shown in green and the highest is in white.

**8**    *Maps that show natural features such as forests or hills are called physical maps.*

## Coastlines

Coastlines can have hachures added to them to give the idea of high cliffs. Shadows can give a similar effect.

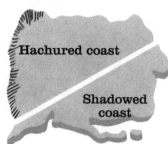

Hachured coast

Shadowed coast

## Sea

The sea can be shown in many ways, such as small blue dots or wavy blue lines. You could show different depths of water by using different shades of blue.

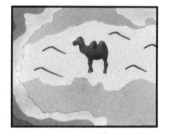

Deep water

Shallow water

## Deserts

You could draw small hills on a yellow background to show dunes in a desert. A symbol, such as a camel or a cactus, will add to the effect.

## Ice and snow

You could use white paint, chalk or white pencil to show areas of ice and snow. Cover the whole area, or draw large, white snowflake symbols to represent snow.

The igloo shows an area that is always under snow.

## Map facts: cartouches

Cartouches are decorated panels containing the title of a map or the key to its symbols. They were first drawn on Italian maps in the 15th century. They often showed flowers, fruit or birds, as well as fancy scrolls and swirls. Sometimes they showed things associated with the map. Navigation maps, for instance, might have shown anchors and ships' wheels.

You can draw cartouches to decorate your own maps. You could make up a simple pattern, or draw pictures associated with the map. You could draw windsurfers on a map of a tourist resort, for instance.

## Treasure map cartouche

This cartouche would suit a pirate's treasure map. It contains drawings of the treasure as well as some things you might encounter on a treasure-hunting expedition.

You can find out how to draw an ancient-style treasure map on pages 16-17. You could include a cartouche like this on your version.

# A bike trail map

For a well-planned bike trail, it is important to have a good map of your route. Before you start to draw, you need to use a good map with contours to find routes that will be enjoyable to cycle. Using the scale on the map, decide how far you want to cycle. Check that the roads are not too hilly or dangerously busy. Varied countryside will make rides more interesting. Roads along ridges, for instance, might give you good views.

## Tracing the route

1. From the map, trace your route on tracing paper. You could trace more than one route. Include landmarks that will be easy to spot.

2. Show where other roads turn off your route. This helps to prevent cyclists taking the wrong turning by mistake.

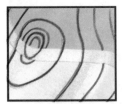

3. Show hills using contours*. If showing each contour makes your map cluttered, then leave out, say, alternate contours.

4. Trace or photocopy your map on plain paper. Then you can decorate it as suggested on the right. You could make several copies, one for each person going on the bike trail.

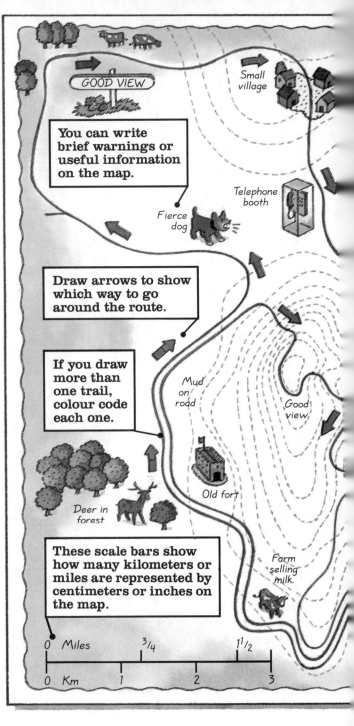

GOOD VIEW

Small village

You can write brief warnings or useful information on the map.

Telephone booth

Fierce dog

Draw arrows to show which way to go around the route.

If you draw more than one trail, colour code each one.

Mud on road

Good view

Old fort

Deer in forest

Farm selling milk.

These scale bars show how many kilometers or miles are represented by centimeters or inches on the map.

0   Miles     ³/₄     1¹/₂

0   Km    1    2    3

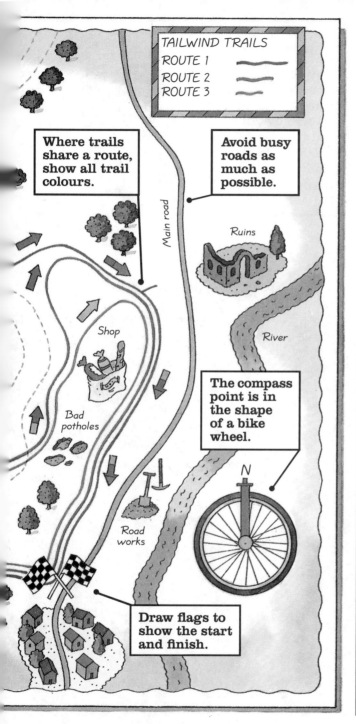

TAILWIND TRAILS
ROUTE 1
ROUTE 2
ROUTE 3

Where trails share a route, show all trail colours.

Avoid busy roads as much as possible.

Main road

Ruins

River

Shop

The compass point is in the shape of a bike wheel.

Bad potholes

N

Road works

Draw flags to show the start and finish.

## How to read contours

Contours connect land of the same height. They are drawn on maps to show where hills are and how steep they are. Contours can also be used to show the depth of water.

If the contours are far apart, the hill slopes gently.

If the contours are close together, the hill is steep.

Reading the contours on the large map, can you figure out which bike trail would suit each group of cyclists in the list on the right? (Answer at bottom of page.)

A  A family with young children.
B  Two fairly fit teenagers.
C  A super-fit athlete.

## Map facts: writing a scale

There are three main ways of writing scales on maps.

**1. Linear scale.** Each section represents the same distance. Routes can easily be measured using this method, shown below.

| 0 | Miles | | 3/4 | | 1 1/2 | | |
| 0 | Km | 1 | | 2 | | 3 | |

**2. Representative fraction.** The first figure is a distance on the map. The second is the real distance it represents. Both figures use the same units.

**3. Written scale.** This scale is simply written out.

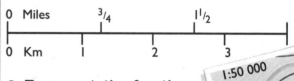

1:50 000

2cm = 1km

2in = 1 mile

Answer: Orange route: group A; Blue route: group B; Red route: group C.

# Old maps

Before printing was invented, maps had to be drawn by hand and painted individually. They were very rare, and often works of art in themselves. This page shows some examples of ancient maps. On the next page you can find out how to make a map of your town that looks as if it was drawn hundreds of years ago.

On the next page you can find out how to make a map of your town

## Map facts: oldest maps

The oldest surviving maps were made around 500BC by the Babylonians from the Middle East. They carved the maps on clay slabs, called tablets.

## Ptolemy's world map

The Greek scholar, Claudius Ptolemy, produced maps of the world in the second century AD. He based his drawings on mathematical calculations, along with information provided by sailors and explorers. According to Ptolemy's information, Europe, Africa and Asia were the only continents in the world. He did not know that America, Australia and Antarctica existed. The map on the right was based on Ptolemy's information.

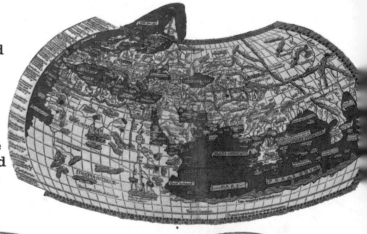

## New discoveries

As new areas were found by Europeans, the places were included on maps. This map was made in 1668. It shows that America and Australia had been discovered. Parts of the world which had not been explored by Europeans at that time are left blank.

## Town map

This map of New York was drawn in 1664, when the city was much smaller than today. The city ends at a wall, which was built to protect citizens from attack. Wall Street now stands on the site of this wall. The map shows drawings of things like buildings and ships. The effect is a cross between a map and a drawing of the sights you would have seen in New York at that time.

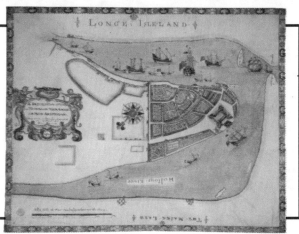

## Old-style town map

To make an old-style map of a town that you know, use a base map of the town as it is today. Trace the busiest streets of the middle of the town, including ancient districts. Then trace the map on a fresh piece of paper, drawing the roads so that they are uneven, like on old maps. Make the buildings look flat and haphazard. Use watercolours in an uneven painting style to add to the old look.

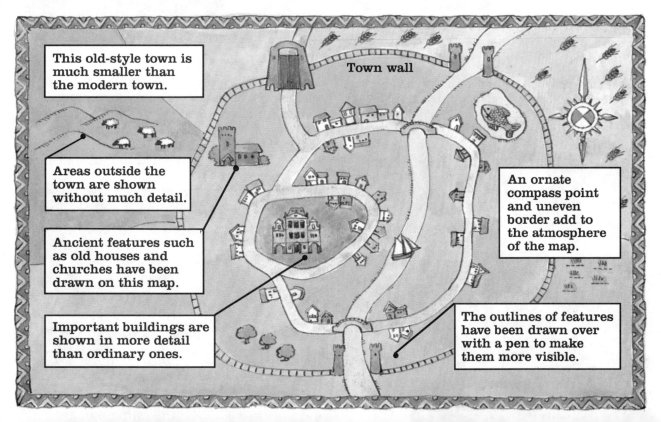

This old-style town is much smaller than the modern town.

Town wall

Areas outside the town are shown without much detail.

Ancient features such as old houses and churches have been drawn on this map.

Important buildings are shown in more detail than ordinary ones.

An ornate compass point and uneven border add to the atmosphere of the map.

The outlines of features have been drawn over with a pen to make them more visible.

# New maps

Today, cartographers have a range of accurate devices which they use to record map details. They can even make maps of things that cannot be seen by the naked eye, such as information about weather or climate changes. The use of satellites, telescopes and space probes has also enabled maps to be made of distant galaxies.*

## Satellite images

Satellites can be used to plot things like landforms and weather conditions. The satellite image on the right shows clouds over part of Europe. The curled cloud is a severe storm.

## Space maps

Here, images of parts of Io, one of Jupiter's moons, were taken by a space probe and joined together. They did not cover the whole area, so the moon looks incomplete.

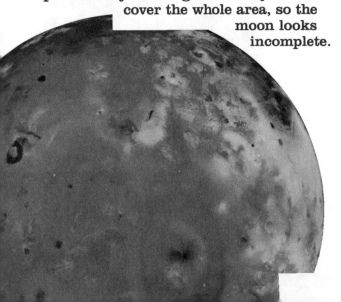

## Star maps

Some satellites orbit the Earth carrying telescopes, which look at distant stars. The results are used to make accurate star maps. In space, telescopes are more powerful than on Earth because they are beyond the haze of the Earth's atmosphere.

The white dot in the middle of the red gas cloud is a star.

*There is more information about how modern maps are made on pages 30-31.

# A picture from space

Satellite photos of places in darkness show towns picked out as clusters of lights. To draw a picture in this style, use thick white poster paint on black paper.

1. Using a base map, trace the outline in pencil. Mark town positions with dots. This map shows Sicily, an Italian island.

2. Place the tracing on the black paper and draw over the outline and the town positions to press them into the paper.

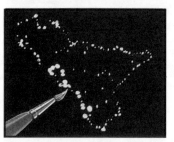

3. Mark the towns and cities with clusters of small white dots. Using thick paint, dab the paint on the paper with the tip of a brush.

4. Make sure that the clusters are similar in size and shape to the original towns and cities on the base map. Leave the sea black.

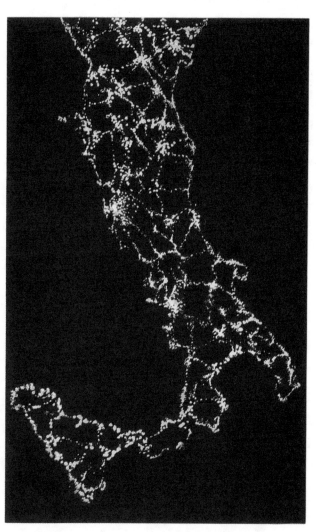

The map above shows both Sicily and Italy. Notice how the dots are so close together in some areas that they merge into large blobs of paint. On the outskirts of towns and cities, the dots are more widely spaced. Towns and cities on the coast help to define the shape of the country.

# A treasure map

Pirates drew maps to remind them where they had hidden their treasure when they returned to collect it, years later. Coded riddles written on the maps indicated where the treasure lay buried. You could make your own treasure map, complete with a riddle.

## Making the map look old

For best results, paint the map on thick watercolor paper. It will absorb the watery paints that you put on it. You can buy paper like this from art shops.

1. Fold your sheet of paper several times until it is a small square. Make sure the creases are all fairly sharp.

2. Unfold the paper and wipe some strong, cold tea over it, using a tea bag or paintbrush. (A thin, watery coat like this is called a wash.)

3. While the paper is damp, paint more patches of tea on parts of the sheet. It does not matter if the paper wrinkles slightly. This will emphasize the old look of the paper.

4. Let the paper dry. You could blot some parts with a tissue, to make them look as if they have faded more than other parts.

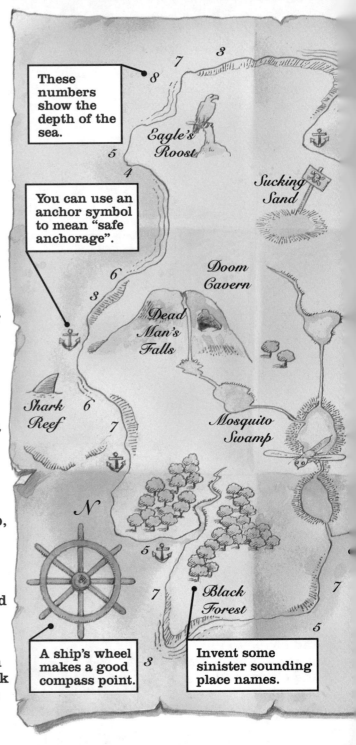

These numbers show the depth of the sea.

You can use an anchor symbol to mean "safe anchorage".

A ship's wheel makes a good compass point.

Invent some sinister sounding place names.

Eagle's Roost

Sucking Sand

Doom Cavern

Dead Man's Falls

Shark Reef

Mosquito Swamp

N

Black Forest

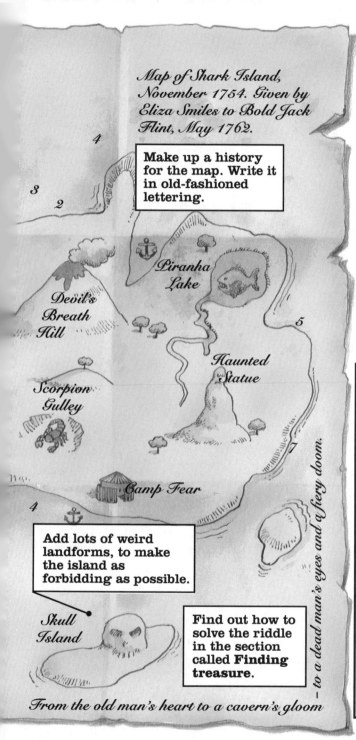

Map of Shark Island, November 1754. Given by Eliza Smiles to Bold Jack Flint, May 1762.

Make up a history for the map. Write it in old-fashioned lettering.

4

3

2

Piranha Lake

Devil's Breath Hill

5

Scorpion Gulley

Haunted Statue

7

Camp Fear

4

Add lots of weird landforms, to make the island as forbidding as possible.

Skull Island

Find out how to solve the riddle in the section called **Finding treasure**.

From the old man's heart to a cavern's gloom – to a dead man's eyes and a fiery doom.

## Drawing the map

The map can be fairly sketchy, as if hastily drawn by a pirate. Drawing it in brown ink will help make the map look old.

1. Draw the outline of the island. (Be careful when going over the creases.) Around the coast, use wavy lines or dots to show the sea.

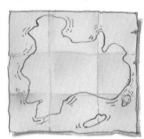

2. Add the mountains, trees, swamps and any other details you like. Give dramatic names to the features.

## Finding treasure

The spot where the pirate's treasure lies is coded to make the treasure more difficult to find. The riddle around the edge tells you how to find the treasure.

The riddle has to be solved to connect two sets of points on the map. The lines cross where the treasure lies.

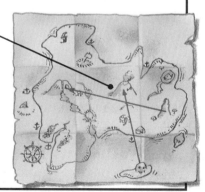

Write a puzzle for your map. Show it to your friends and let them try to locate the treasure.

# World maps

All world maps are distorted, because it is impossible to show the whole of the Earth's curve accurately on a flat map. Differently distorted views of the world, called projections, can be created. The two projections below were created by the same cartographer over a hundred years ago.

## Equal area projection

In this projection, the sizes of areas of land are correct in relation to each other. However, the shape of most of the land is distorted.

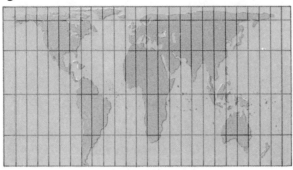

## Accurate shape projection

This projection is useful for giving an idea of the shapes of areas of land. It is not accurate for showing the relative sizes of areas of land.

## Map facts: latitude and longitude

A grid of numbered lines, called latitude and longitude lines, are drawn on world maps. They divide the world into imaginary sections. They can help people to find places on the map.

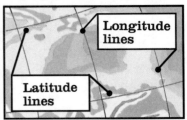

Longitude lines

Latitude lines

The maps on the left are marked with latitude and longitude lines. The line positions are different on each map, owing to the different projections.

## A cut-up globe

The most accurate way to show the world on flat paper is to show it as strips peeled from a globe. A map of this kind is very tricky to read, though, because gaps are left between parts of the world. The picture on the right shows curved strips peeled from a globe and laid out flat, to make a map of the world.

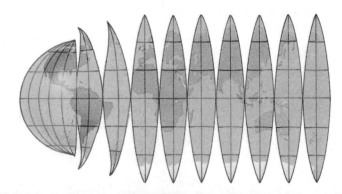

# Wildlife map of the world

This map shows wildlife from some regions of the world. You could draw a version of it, showing any animals you choose. Copy them from pictures in books or magazines, on a separate piece of paper.

Then cut them out and stick them on the map. You may want to make a bigger map so that you can display it on a wall. At the bottom of the page, you can see how to enlarge the wildlife map.*

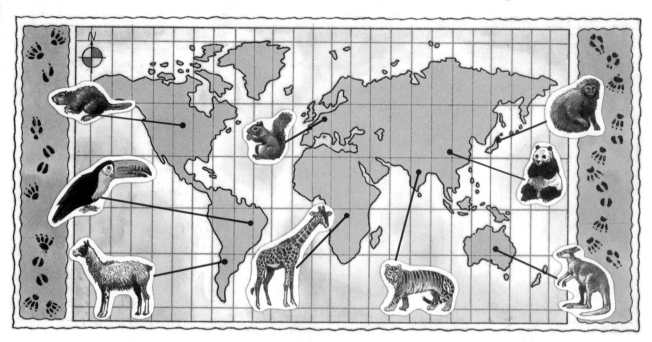

## How to enlarge the wildlife map

**1.** Copy the lines of latitude and longitude from the map above. Space all lines twice as far apart.

**2.** Together, the lines will form a grid of boxes. Now copy the map box by box into your grid, in pencil.

**3.** When you have copied the map, draw over the outlines of the landforms with a pen to make them permanent.

**4.** Finally, decorate the map and add a compass point. You could add a patterned border if you want one.

*There are more ideas for maps to put on your wall on pages 22-23.

# A fantasy map

It can be fun to invent a fantasy map full of odd mythical creatures such as trolls, and hazards such as bottomless marshes. An element of mystery can be added to the map by including coded place names. You could use this map as inspiration for your own maps or you could draw a map based on an existing fantasy story.

## Map details

Try to include details which add to the overall atmosphere of the map. You could start by making the paper look old, following the technique shown on page 16.

## Using colors

Use colors to help convey whether an area is safe or not. For example, use warm, light shades to indicate friendly areas. Cold, dingy shades are good for showing hostile areas.

## Coded alphabet

Each rune-like letter below corresponds to a letter of the alphabet. Try figuring out the place names on the map.

A B C D  E F G H  I J K L M N O P Q R S T  U V W X  Y Z

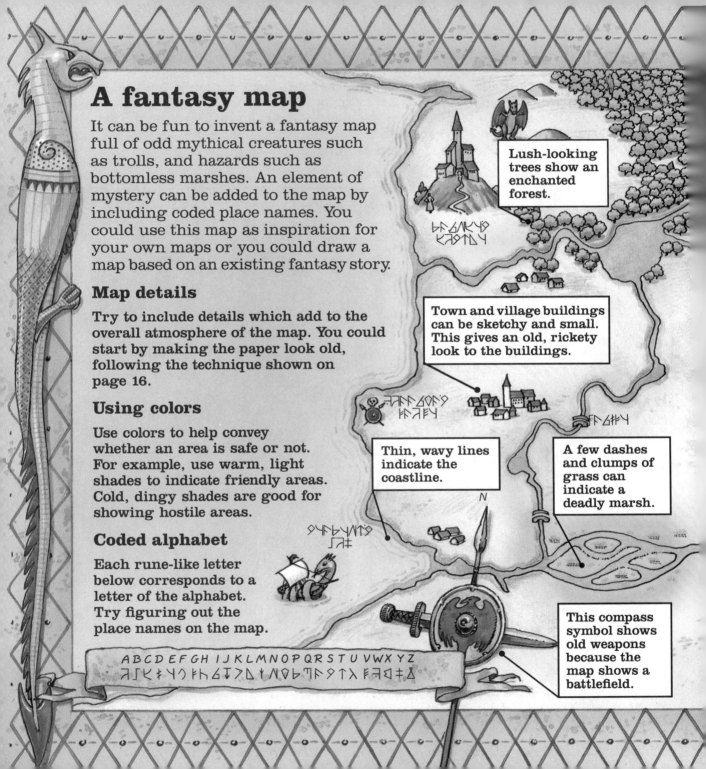

Lush-looking trees show an enchanted forest.

Town and village buildings can be sketchy and small. This gives an old, rickety look to the buildings.

Thin, wavy lines indicate the coastline.

A few dashes and clumps of grass can indicate a deadly marsh.

This compass symbol shows old weapons because the map shows a battlefield.

N

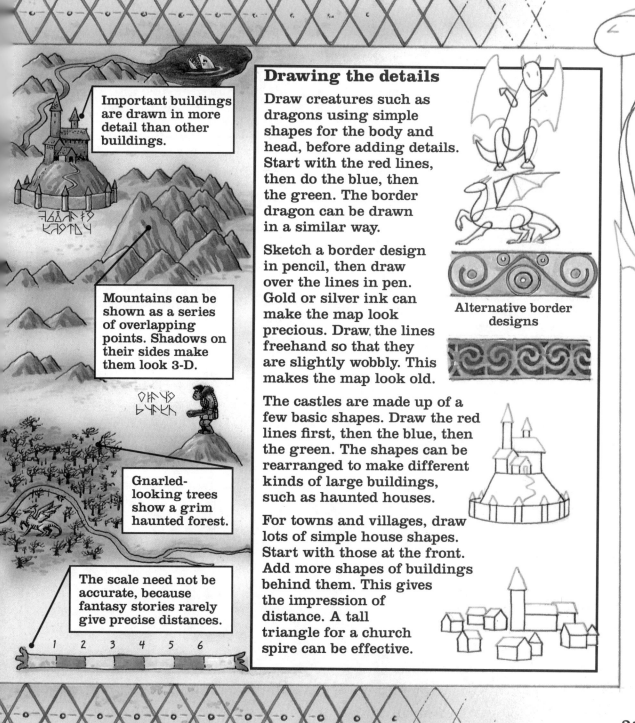

**Important buildings are drawn in more detail than other buildings.**

**Mountains can be shown as a series of overlapping points. Shadows on their sides make them look 3-D.**

**Gnarled-looking trees show a grim haunted forest.**

**The scale need not be accurate, because fantasy stories rarely give precise distances.**

1 2 3 4 5 6

## Drawing the details

Draw creatures such as dragons using simple shapes for the body and head, before adding details. Start with the red lines, then do the blue, then the green. The border dragon can be drawn in a similar way.

Sketch a border design in pencil, then draw over the lines in pen. Gold or silver ink can make the map look precious. Draw the lines freehand so that they are slightly wobbly. This makes the map look old.

Alternative border designs

The castles are made up of a few basic shapes. Draw the red lines first, then the blue, then the green. The shapes can be rearranged to make different kinds of large buildings, such as haunted houses.

For towns and villages, draw lots of simple house shapes. Start with those at the front. Add more shapes of buildings behind them. This gives the impression of distance. A tall triangle for a church spire can be effective.

# Maps for your wall

You can make large versions of maps, such as the ones in this book, to put on your wall. By decorating them in different ways you can use your wall maps to show a variety of information. These pages show you how to enlarge your maps to poster size and give you ideas on how to decorate them.

## Increasing the size of a map

Draw a grid of squares on tracing paper, spacing each line by 1in (or 2cm). Make your grid big enough to cover the map that you want to show. Stick the grid on the map using adhesive tape*.

On a large piece of cardboard, draw an enlarged grid in pencil, with the same number of squares as the original. To make the map twice as big, space the lines of the grid twice as far apart.

Copy the map square by square on the cardboard. Then erase the grid. Finally, decorate the map. Use bright felt-tips, so that you can see the map clearly from a distance when it is on the wall.

## Weather map

You could make weather symbols to stick on a map, like those shown below. Reposition your symbols every day, according to the weather forecasts.*

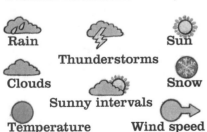

Rain

Thunderstorms

Sun

Clouds

Sunny intervals

Snow

Temperature

Wind speed

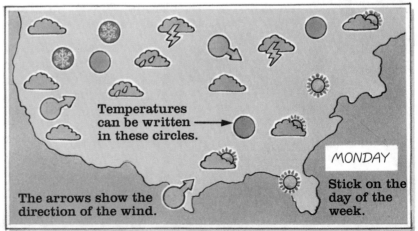

Temperatures can be written in these circles.

The arrows show the direction of the wind.

MONDAY

Stick on the day of the week.

*Use removable adhesive tape to stick grids and symbols over the maps. That way, you will not ruin the maps when you peel them off.

# World events map

On an outline map of the world, you could highlight any areas where important events happen. Use symbols like the ones below to show events. Color the countries where events happen.

War

Election

International conference

Hurricane

Sports event

Volcano

Earthquake

Famine

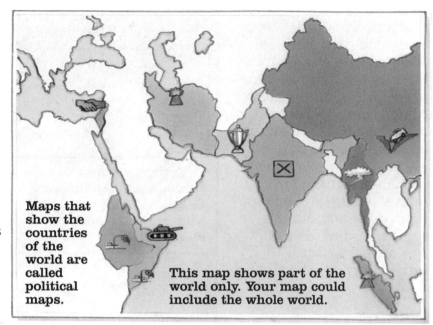

Maps that show the countries of the world are called political maps.

This map shows part of the world only. Your map could include the whole world.

# Tourist map

You could draw a map of an area that you visited on your travels. Using simple symbols, indicate the places that you visited and the things that you did during your stay.

Swimming

Sunbathing

Windsurfing

Forest trail

Museum

Town

Restaurant

Shops

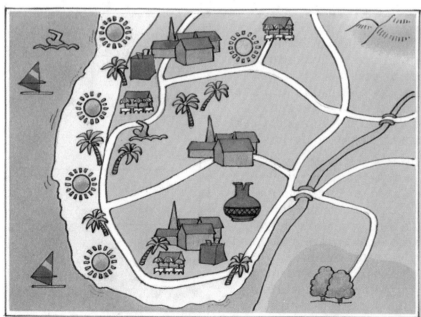

# Diagram and pattern maps

Maps need not represent every detail of an area. They can be made to look like diagrams. This is useful for route maps, for instance, where a complicated network can be simplified to make it easier to read, as shown on this page. On the opposite page are maps drawn in particular styles. Maps like them are often used in advertisements because they are eye-catching.

## Making a route map

Most transport systems have route maps. The routes are simplified so that people can follow them easily. They are also color coded so that they can be distinguished. The straight lines between stops do not represent real distances to scale.

Follow the steps on this page to make a clear route map of an imaginary transport system for your area. If you show more than one type of transport, you could think up different ways to draw this on your map. Use broken lines for train routes, for instance.

## Drawing the map

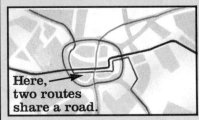

Here, two routes share a road.

**1. Trace your network from a map of your area. Use a different colour for each route, to make them stand out from each other.**

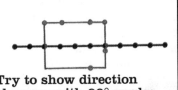

Try to show direction changes with 90° angles.

**4. Redraw a second route, starting with the stops that it shares with the simplest route. Space out other stops evenly.**

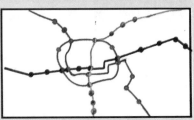

**2. Mark where you want stops to be on each route. You could mark stops near a variety of places, such as shops or a school.**

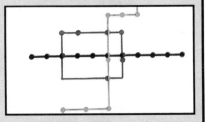

**5. Draw in all routes. You may need to draw several versions, adjusting the positions of the stops, until it all fits together.**

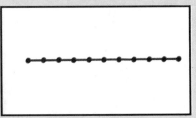

**3. Redraw the simplest route, making its shape more diagrammatic and regular. Make spaces equal between each stop.**

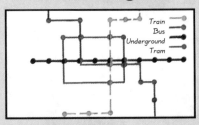

**6. Draw a final version of the map. Use felt-tips to make the route map clear and bright. Draw a key to the routes at the side.**

## Grid map

To draw a stylized, angular map like this, follow these steps.

1. Trace the outline of an area from a base map, using pencil.

2. Lay your tracing over a piece of graph paper. Using a fine ink pen, redraw the map following the graph lines that are closest to the map outline.

3. Erase the pencil lines made by your tracing of the base map. Finally, color the grid map, using bright felt-tips.

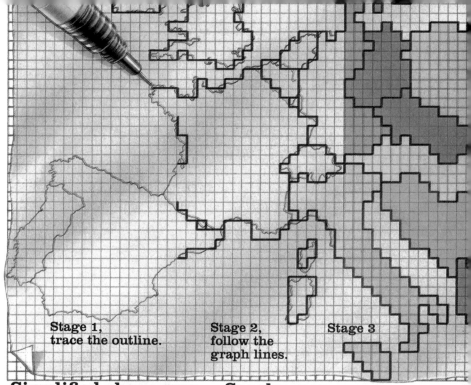

Stage 1, trace the outline.

Stage 2, follow the graph lines.

Stage 3

## Circuit diagram map

An electricity company might use a map like this in an advertisement. First, draw a simplified pencil outline of the area you want to show.

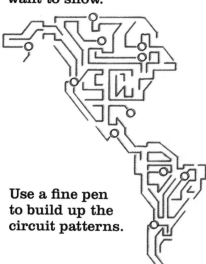

Use a fine pen to build up the circuit patterns.

## Simplified shape map

The outlines of countries or continents can be made into striking shapes by simplifying the shapes of borders into a series of straight lines.

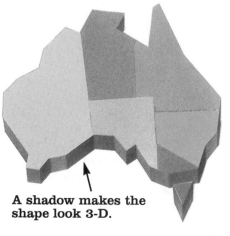

A shadow makes the shape look 3-D.

## Spooky map

Adapt the basic shape of a country to draw a spooky map like this one. Look for parts of coastline that could become fiendish faces, with parts that drip blood.

# Thematic maps

Maps can show information which compares numbers and amounts of things. This is called statistical information. These kinds of maps are known as thematic maps. The thematic maps below compare statistics by showing numbers as a collection of squares.

## Number maps

This map shows how many people live in each of the regions of the world. Each region's population has been converted into a number of squares. On the map, the shapes of the regions are recognizable compared to their real geographical shapes.

You could draw a similar map of your home, comparing the time you spend in each room over 24 hours. The rooms in which you spend the most time will be the biggest.

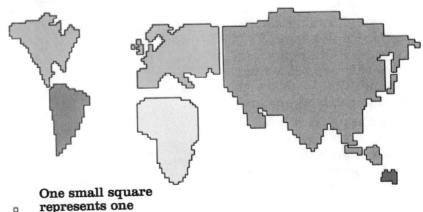

One small square represents one million people.

North America
429 squares

South America
302 squares

Europe
791 squares

Africa
677 squares

Asia
3186 squares

Australasia
27 squares

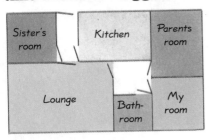

| ROOM | TIME | SQUARES |
|---|---|---|
| My room | 9 hrs | 36 |
| Parents' room | 0 hrs | – |
| Kitchen | 45 mins | 3 |
| Bathroom | 1 hr | 4 |
| Lounge | 3 hrs | 12 |
| Sister's room | 1 hr 30 mins | 6 |
| Out of house | 8 hrs 45 mins | – |

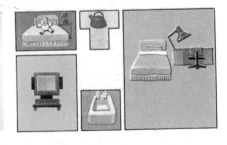

First, draw a floor plan of your home. The sizes of the rooms don't need to be accurately drawn to scale, since their sizes will be distorted later.

Write down how long you spend in each room. Using one square to represent fifteen minutes, calculate how many squares represent each room.

Draw the finished map on graph paper. The distorted floor plan reflects the amount of time spent in each room. Symbols show what the room is used for.

# Castle game

You could use a floor plan as the base for a game. This plan shows a haunted castle with secret passages. In the game, characters race around the castle collecting objects. You could invent a plan, or trace this one, enlarge it on a photocopier* and color it in.

## The pieces

Name the characters, such as Black Princess or Red Magician, and invent objects to find. Draw the pieces with felt-tips on paper and cut them out.

## Playing the game

Put an object in each room except the Dungeon. Throw a die to move. If you land on a yellow door, you can enter the room to pick up the object. You can go in one door and out through another. You can move to any room if you land on a red trap door, but in return, throw the dice to take a risk (see top right). When all the other objects have been picked up, race to the Treasure Chest. The game ends when this is collected. The best score wins.

*You can use photocopiers in public libraries.

Color code the pieces to show their values: pink = 4, yellow = 2.

Put the Treasure Chest in the Turret Room. It is worth six points.

Draw corridors, made up of equal squares, to move along.

### Risks

| | |
|---|---|
| Send a player back to Start. | ⚀ |
| Spook locks you in. Miss a turn. | ⚁ |
| Ghost gives you the Goblet. | ⚂ |
| Drop one of your objects. | ⚃ |
| Go to Kitchens for a snack. | ⚄ |
| Get chained up in Dungeon. Miss two turns. | ⚅ |

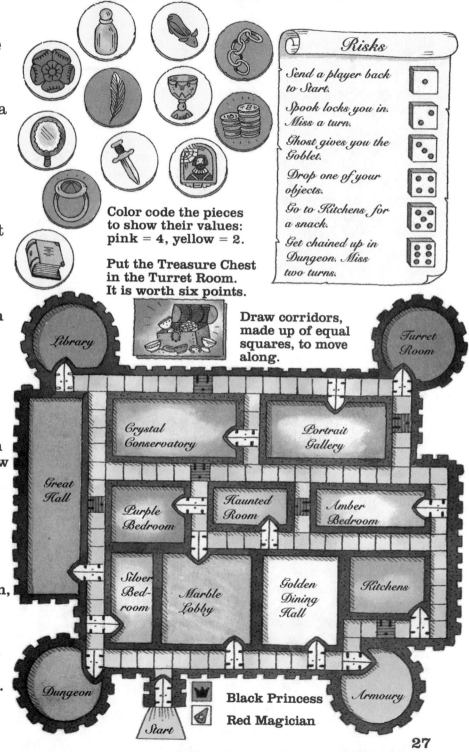

27

# Statistical charts

Statistical charts are ways of showing pieces of information so that they can be understood at a glance. Graphs are a type of statistical chart. On this page, you can see how to make a bar chart. On the opposite page, you can find out how to make graphs.

## Collecting information

Before you draw your chart, decide what information you want to show, then make a list of the things you need to find out. For instance, for a chart showing how people get to school, your list could look like the one on the right.

| How do you get to school? | Total |
| --- | --- |
| Walk | 7 |
| By car | 6 |
| By bike | 7 |
| By bus | 5 |
| By train | 2 |

## Bar charts

Bar charts compare amounts of things. To construct a bar chart, draw straight lines across the bottom and up the side of a sheet of paper. Mark evenly-spaced units up the vertical line. On this chart, one unit stands for one person. If the numbers of people were greater, one unit could stand for, say, five people.

Choose a width for the bars. Draw each bar so that it lines up with the number of people that it represents. Decorate the bars so that they are in keeping with the information that they show. Finally, write on the bars what each of them represents and give your bar chart a title.

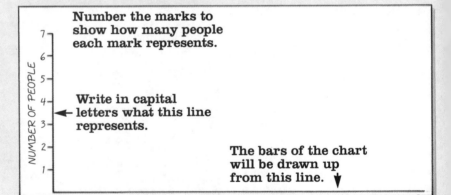

Number the marks to show how many people each mark represents.

NUMBER OF PEOPLE

← Write in capital letters what this line represents.

The bars of the chart will be drawn up from this line. ↓

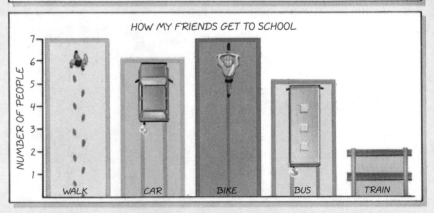

HOW MY FRIENDS GET TO SCHOOL

NUMBER OF PEOPLE

WALK    CAR    BIKE    BUS    TRAIN

## Graphs

Like other charts, graphs show information as a diagram, rather than as a list of statistics. Graphs are used to show the relationship between two changing quantities. As an example, you could plot a graph of the time you take to complete a car journey, compared with the distance you travel during the journey.

### Collecting information

You will need to collect statistics before you plot the graph. For a graph of a car journey, note the distance every five minutes of your trip.

During the journey, write down any notable parts of the trip, such as when you go fast or are held up.

| Minutes | Distance | Comments |
|---------|----------|----------|
| 5 | 5 | Fast, straight road |
| 10 | 12 | |
| 15 | 21 | |
| 20 | 27 | Slow, twisting road |
| 25 | 28 | |
| 30 | 30 | |
| 35 | 30 | Road works |
| 40 | 35 | Arrived at lake |

## Drawing the graph

Draw straight lines, called axes, across the bottom and up the side of the paper. Then mark off units of time and distance on the lines. Directly above each time unit, draw a dot level with the distance you had reached by that time.

When you have marked each of the dots you can connect them, using a ruler. To make the graph more attractive, you could decorate it with symbols which show the most important events of your journey, such as the things you noted down.

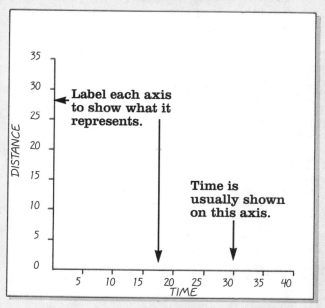

Label each axis to show what it represents.

Time is usually shown on this axis.

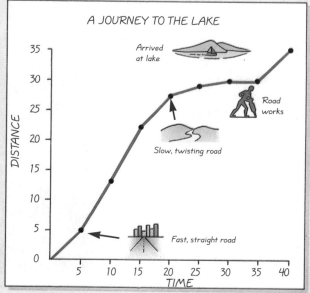

A JOURNEY TO THE LAKE

29

# Modern cartography

On these two pages, you can find out how professional cartographers produce their maps. Map production relies on very advanced equipment and technology. However, the cartographer's skill in putting the map together is still an important part of the process.

## Gathering information

This aerial photo shows details of a town.

The map was drawn using the aerial photo as a guide.

Before drawing a map, cartographers need to know all the information which is relevant to their map. They research the area thoroughly and study any existing base maps of it.

Surveyors visit the area to note details about what is on the ground. For a town map, buildings are plotted and angles of streets measured. For a relief map, heights of hills are measured.

Aerial photographs (photographs taken from high above, looking down) are valuable to cartographers. They provide a bird's eye view of the land and help match up the position of landmarks.

## Modern technology

Modern technology, such as satellite imagery and radar, helps cartographers to gather information without actually going to a place and measuring it. This technique is called remote sensing. Cartographers use computers to store and analyze the masses of information that they collect.

Satellites take pictures of the Earth's atmosphere and its surface. From these, weather maps and maps of the Earth's surface are made. The satellite photo on the left is of San Francisco. It shows clear details, such as the coastline, the nearby mountain ranges and bridges across the bay.

## Making the map

Once the information has been gathered, the cartographers decide how the map should look. For example, a tourist map will have more pictures than a map for pilots. The cartographers also need to choose a scale*. For world, continental and national maps, they also choose a projection*. Lettering must be clear and suit the theme of the map. Different type styles and sizes are used for different features.

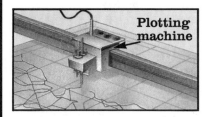

Plotting machine

A cartographic technician feeds measurements of the map outline and positions of the features into a computer. These are then drawn by a plotting machine.

Scribing

The features of the map may be drawn on paper. For higher quality maps, the features are scraped out from plastic-coated film. This is called scribing.

Sticking on lettering

Lettering is typed into a computer and printed on film, which is then stuck over the map. On some maps, lettering and detail, such as shading, may also be drawn by hand.

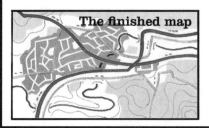

The finished map

Many cartographers draw their maps bigger than necessary so that they can include more detail. The maps are then reduced to the correct size when they are printed.

## Map drawing tools

As well as computers, cartographers use special tools and equipment, such as those shown below, to produce fine lines and accurate drawings.

Technical pens draw very smooth, regular lines.

Calligraphy pens are useful for decorative lettering.

Protractors help to draw accurate angles.

Scale rules are used for measuring distances on maps. They have several different scales.

Transfer lettering, symbols, lines and shapes may be used.

*For more about scale, see page 4. For more about projections, see page 18.

# Index

Ancient Babylonian map (page 12) courtesy of the British Museum.
Antique Ptolemy map and map of the world (page 12) courtesy of Jonathan Potter Ltd.
Antique map of New York (page 13) courtesy of the British Library.
Satellite image of Europe (page 14) courtesy of European Space Agency/Science Photo Library.
Space image of Io (page 14) courtesy of NASA.

Space photograph of star nebula (page 14) courtesy of S. Heap, NASA/Goddard Space Flight Center.
Aerial photograph of Wolverhampton (page 30) courtesy of Wolverhampton Metropolitan Borough Council.
Satellite image of San Francisco (page 30) courtesy of Earth Satellite Corporation/Science Photo Library.
Information and picture references (page 31) provided by Ordnance Survey.

ISBN 0-590-47996-2
Copyright © 1993 by Usborne Publishing Ltd. All rights reserved.
Published by Scholastic Inc., 555 Broadway, New York, NY 10012, by arrangement with Usborne Publishing Ltd.
12 11 10 9 8                                    6 7 8 9/9
Printed in the U.S.A.                                    23
First Scholastic printing, February 1994